ALLEN IVERSON

Glen Macnow

—SPORTS GREAT BOOKS—

Enslow Publishers, Inc.

40 Industrial Road   PO Box 38
Box 398   Aldershot
Berkeley Heights, NJ 07922   Hants GU12 6BP
USA   UK
http://www.enslow.com

Dedicated to Anthony L. Gargano,
the world's greatest Philadelphia 76ers fan.
Yo, Cuz, you make it fun every day.

Library of Congress Cataloging-in-Publication Data

Macnow, Glen.
  Sports great : Allen Iverson / Glen Macnow.
     p. cm. — (Sports great books)
Includes index.
Summary: Profiles professional basketball star Allen Iverson, whose
speed and determination helped him to overcome his relatively small
stature to earn the All-Star MVP trophy and the NBA's Most Valuable
Player award in 2001.
  ISBN 0-7660-2063-0
1. Iverson, Allen, 1975—-Juvenile literature. 2. Basketball
players—United States—Biography—Juvenile literature. [1. Iverson,
Allen, 1975- 2. Basketball players. 3. African Americans—Biography.]
I. Title. II. Series.
GV884.I84 M33 2003
796.323'092—dc21

                                        2002005500

Printed in the United States of America

10 9 8 7 6 5 4 3 2 1

To Our Readers:
We have done our best to make sure all Internet Addresses in this book were active and
appropriate when we went to press. However, the author and the publisher have no
control over and assume no liability for the material available on those Internet sites or
on other Web sites they may link to. Any comments or suggestions can be sent by e-mail
to comments@enslow.com or to the address on the back cover.

Illustration Credits: Andrew Bernstein/NBAE/Getty Images, p. 11; Andy Hayt
NBA/Allsport, p. 29; Andy Lyons/Allsport, p. 45; Donald Miralle/Allsport,
p. 59; Fernando Medina/NBAE/Getty Images, p. 49; Jason Wice/Allsport,
p. 37; Jennifer Pottheiser/NBAE/Getty Images, p. 55; Jesse Garrabrant/
NBAE/Getty Images, pp. 13, 30, 31, 35, 47; Jonathan Daniel/Allsport, pp. 1, 17,
57; Ken Levine/Allsport, p. 23; M. David leeds/Allsport, pp. 8, 53; Mitchell
Layton/NBAE/Getty Images, p. 21; Stephen Dunn/Allsport, p. 39; Vincent
Laforet/Allsport, p. 44.

Cover Illustration: Jonathan Daniel/Allsport.

Contents

Chapter 1

A New Star

He is pro basketball's most fascinating player. And, he is its most misunderstood. Who exactly is Allen Iverson?

Start with 165 pounds of raw energy. The game begins and Iverson is juking and slicing and leaping past opponents. Monsters twice his size knock this little man to the floor, but he gets up, rubs the pain out of his body, and calmly sinks two free throws.

The National Basketball Association (NBA) is loaded with blazing-fast athletes. But none can keep up with Allen Ezail Iverson. Is he the quickest in history? "I don't know, I didn't play against everybody in history," he says. "But I haven't seen anyone yet who can catch me."

Bragging? Perhaps. But he has earned that right. Twice, Allen Iverson—all five feet ten inches of him—has led the NBA in scoring. In 2001, he was voted the top player in the league's All-Star Game. A few months later, he was named the Most Valuable Player for the season after taking the Philadelphia 76ers to the NBA Finals.

On this night in June 2001, the Sixers are playing the Los Angeles Lakers in Game 1 of the Finals. No one thinks the Sixers have a chance against the Lakers, who are led by superstar guard Kobe Bryant and 320-pound center Shaquille O'Neal.

Allen Iverson slashes between defenders David Robinson and Michael Finley and sinks a layup during the NBA All-Star Game on February 11, 2001.

No one, perhaps, but the Sixers themselves.

Iverson is guarded by Tyronn Lue, a pesky little guard who is playing him so close he seems to be inside Iverson's pocket. No problem. Allen Iverson works his famous crossover move. He dribbles at the top of the key, bouncing the ball in front of Lue's eyes. Suddenly, Iverson dribbles to the left. His head and shoulders dip. Lue lunges for it. Mistake! Iverson dribbles right. With his quick step, he is gone. He flashes through the paint for an easy layup.

He scores 30 points in the game's first half. Lakers coach Phil Jackson tries guarding Iverson with three different players. None can do the job. The Sixers win 107–101. Iverson finishes with 45 points, including a game-clinching 18-footer in overtime.

The Lakers go on to win the series and the NBA title in 2001. But on this one night, anyway, Iverson and his teammates are the kings of the basketball world.

After the game, Iverson sits in the locker room surrounded by cameramen and reporters. He slouches on a stool in exhaustion. Naked, except for a towel, his dozens of tattoos are on display for all to see. His hair is fashioned in cornrows. His voice is a barely audible mumble—partly from fatigue, and partly from his dislike of answering reporters' questions.

Iverson's appearance and manners bother many people. He has seen his share of trouble—from growing up in a drug-infested neighborhood to spending time in jail as a teen for his role in a bowling-alley brawl. Some critics see him as everything wrong with modern-day athletes.

But listen to his words.

"I play every game like it's my last," he said. "I owe that much to myself. I owe it to my family and friends. I owe it to the sport and to God, for giving me the talent. A lot of guys say that but don't mean it. But I'm someone who does because I know a lot of things can happen."

His friends are the guys he grew up with in poverty. Some are tough. Some have been in trouble with the law. They have been called his "posse," but he calls them "Crew Thick." There has been constant talk that they will drag him into trouble. At least one NBA official suggested that Iverson drop the crew for more polished friends.

But Iverson is all about loyalty. Abandon his pals? The same group that saw him through tough times and kept him from trouble more than once? Unthinkable. If Iverson is now riding high, he wants his friends riding along.

His family, too. Iverson and his wife, Tawanna, have two young children, Tiaura and Allen II. The boy, called Deuce, has cornrows like his dad, and is a crowd favorite in Philadelphia. As soon as the game ends, Iverson sweeps his children into his arms. "Being a player is great," he said. "But being a father, that's even better."

In truth, Iverson prefers the company of children. Even now, he is in no hurry to be an adult. He has always felt that adults are too quick to judge him. They look at his baggy, hip-hop clothes, they hear his mumbling voice—but they do not seem to pay attention to what he says.

Kids, on the other hand, are drawn to this new-style star. They see him "keeping it real," as Iverson likes to say. That is one big reason that Iverson's trademark sneaker, made by Reebok, has been the biggest seller in the nation.

"He is the future of the NBA," said Reebok spokesman Dave Fogelson. "Adults really don't relate to him, but kids do."

In many ways, however, Allen Iverson is not very different from the NBA greats who came before him. Like the great Lakers guard Jerry West, he is as tough as a rhino. In his day, West played through injuries big and small. Bouncing off the big men and getting knocked to the floor a dozen times a game was perfectly normal. That is Iverson's game, too.

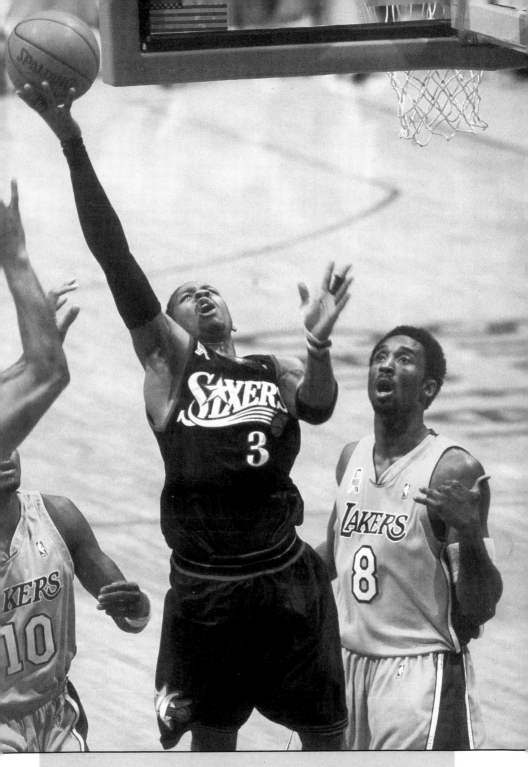

Allen Iverson puts up a shot while the Lakers' Kobe Bryant (8) looks on.

Like Michael Jordan, Iverson has nights when he can carry the entire offense. A 50-point playoff game? Been there, done that. Lead his team by dishing off to another hot man? If that is what has to be done to win. Jordan could not be guarded. He could not be imitated. His No. 23 Bulls jersey was the top seller in the world. These days, it is Iverson's No. 3 Sixers jersey that tops the sales charts.

Like Magic Johnson of the Lakers, Iverson has an ear-to-ear smile that cameras love. Magic had a joy for the game, and anyone playing with him (or watching him) picked up on that joy. He hugged his teammates, his coach, even an occasional fan. The game was supposed to be fun, and Magic played it that way. That is Allen Iverson, as well.

Underneath the smiles and hugs, though, there is a history of pain. Many professional athletes come from poor backgrounds. Few come from poverty as grueling as did Iverson. He spent his youth in a tiny, unheated apartment where there was barely room to tie his shoes. His neighborhood in Hampton, Virginia, is as tough as it gets. The tough times made him grow up fast. But they also left him vulnerable. Sometimes, he closes up in public. He does not want to be hurt again. He is very cautious around strangers.

With friends and relatives, however, he is the class clown. He can capture almost anyone's voice and mannerisms—from TV stars to his coach, Larry Brown. Sometimes, Coach Brown will speak to the Sixers and then leave the room. Iverson will then stand in front of his teammates and imitate the coach, leaving the other players in stitches.

He is also a talented cartoonist. When his basketball days are over, Iverson wants to produce a daily comic strip. "I want it to be funny, but I also want it to tell things the way they really are," he said. "I want it to be for little kids who don't grow up in mansions. They need to know that they're important, too."

Iverson takes a pass during a game against the Detroit Pistons at the First Union Center in Philadelphia on November 21, 2001.

Iverson has tried to express himself in other ways. In 2000, he recorded a rap album under the name "Jewelz." The words were rough and sometimes dirty. After thinking about it (and after being lectured by NBA Commissioner David Stern), Iverson decided not to release the album.

For now, he is all about playing basketball. During his first six seasons, the 76ers grew from being one of the league's worst teams to a challenger for the title. In 2001–02, they had a strong cast: Center Dikembe Mutombo was a defensive star; point guard Eric Snow was a great distributor; sixth man Aaron McKie was a player who could fill almost any role on the floor. Add newcomers Derrick Coleman and Matt Harpring to the mix and the Sixers seemed poised to make another championship run.

The key man, of course, is the smallest one on the court.

It is November 2001. The Sixers's record is just 5–5 after ten games. All five losses came without Iverson, who missed the season's start following elbow surgery. Tonight, against the Detroit Pistons, Iverson is just getting back into form.

As the Pistons rush back, Iverson sees their defense as Swiss cheese: full of holes. He shifts his speed up another gear. He slices around Detroit guard Jerry Stackhouse and slashes past center Ben Wallace. Suddenly, he is at the rim. Finger-roll. Two points.

Next time down the court, the Pistons defense tightens to prevent him from attacking the rim. No problem. Iverson fakes the drive and then stops so quickly that defender Dana Barros nearly rolls over his own ankles. Iverson launches an arcing 18-footer. Bingo. Two more points.

For the rest of the night, Iverson treats fans to a variety of shots. He dunks with ease in the open court. He soars close to the rim for layups. He shoots jumpers up near the rafters. His hang-time is off the charts.

Iverson finishes the game with 38 points. Three Pistons who tried to guard him had to leave with foul trouble. The Sixers win the game, 94–89. Clearly, Iverson seems over his elbow problems.

"The little guy was amazing tonight," Sixers coach Larry Brown said afterward. "Coming off an injury like he had, to play this well is unbelievable. I'm not sure people fully appreciate what he puts into every game."

To fully appreciate what Allen Iverson is today, you have to first look at where he has been.

Chapter 2

Growing Up

Allen Ezail Iverson was born in the small town of Hampton, Virginia, on June 7, 1975. His mother, Anne, was just fifteen at the time. She gave her baby the nickname "Bubba Chuck," after her two favorite uncles. His father, Allen Broughton, was a high school student and a leader in a gang called the Family Connection. His parents split up before Allen was even born.

He grew up poor, sharing a two-bedroom house with thirteen cousins, aunts, and uncles. He needed to wear shoes, day or night, because the floor might be coated with raw sewage. One time the sewer pipe that ran under the house ruptured. The smell was terrible. Often there was no power, because Allen's mother could not afford to pay the bill. No heat, either—another unpaid bill.

And he grew up fast. When Allen was just three years old, his mother told him, "You're the man of the house. You've got to do whatever you need to become a man." In the coming years, Anne Iverson gave birth to two daughters. Allen, not yet even a teenager, knew it was on him to get his family out of their dark, freezing sewer of a home.

"I knew I had to succeed for them," he later said.

The way out of poverty, he decided, would be sports.

Allen moved back in—but he had changed. He realized that his life could be better than a messy house with broken pipes and no rules. If his mom would not discipline him, he would have to discipline himself.

"I had a bigger picture for my life," he said. "I wasn't going to spend my life in the sewer." He had seen enough trouble. Eight of Iverson's friends were killed over the years. One was his best friend, Tony Clark, who had always stood up for Allen whenever he was in trouble.

At Bethel High School, Allen quickly became a star at both basketball and football. Sometimes, he even combined the sports. Folks around Hampton still marvel at how the scrawny teen used to be able to dribble a football as others would dribble a basketball.

Allen played quarterback and safety for the football team, and also returned six kickoffs for touchdowns in his junior year. He led his school to the state championship. In the title game, he passed for 201 yards, ran a punt for a 60-yard touchdown, and intercepted two passes.

Three days later, he scored 37 points in the basketball season opener. That season, he led Bethel High to the state basketball title. He averaged 31.6 points per game.

Parade magazine named him the top high school basketball player in the country and one of the top ten football players. He was the most recognized person in Hampton.

Then trouble found Allen Iverson.

In February 1993, when he was seventeen, Allen and some pals went to a bowling alley on a Saturday night. They rolled a few games, ate some burgers, and shouted a bit too loud. The lane's owner told them to pipe down, but the boys kept making noise. Allen went to the snack bar to order some food. There, he was approached by a group of young men.

As Allen tells the story, the men—all white—began using racial slurs. One challenged him to a fight. Before

Allen could even respond, one of his friends jumped in. Fists and angry words started flying. By most accounts, about forty teens and young men started brawling. Half were African American, half were white. The melee broke down along racial lines.

Allen insists that a friend quickly pulled him out of the brawl and took him home. Others tell a different story of that night. Two people testified that Allen picked up a chair and threw it. The chair hit a young woman in the head, sending her to the hospital.

A videotape taken of the incident never shows Allen in the mob. Still, police later arrested four teens—all African American. Allen Iverson, Virginia's top high school athlete, was one of them. Aside from a traffic ticket, he had never before been in trouble with the law.

The teens were charged with "maiming by mob," which basically means injuring someone during a riot. Many in the community expected charges to be dropped. After all, dozens of people were involved in the fight. Why focus on just four of them?

Still, the four went to trial and were convicted. Even then, most people figured they would get probation (meaning no jail time) and perhaps have to perform public service as their penalty. Instead, Judge Nelson Overton sent Allen and the others to prison for three years.

"I sat in court listening to people lie and there was nothing I could do about it," Allen Iverson recalled. He was sent to prison at the Newport News City Farm, where he lay in bed at night, crying. "I cried about what people said and wrote about me. But, really, they made me stronger."

Public outcry over the jail sentence reached Virginia Governor L. Douglas Wilder. The governor studied the case and ordered Allen released after four months. There

THAT'S MY
BOY
#3 IVERSON

GNWORKS
0-916-2437

Allen Iverson's mother, Anne, cheers him on during a game against the Washington Wizards at the MCI Center in Washington, D.C., in January 2002.

was one condition, however: Allen was not allowed to play organized sports until he graduated from high school.

Two years later, Allen's conviction was reversed by another judge. That judge said there was never enough evidence to find him guilty. Today, there is not a speck of the case on Iverson's record. But the scars remain inside of him.

One good thing did happen in prison. Allen made a new friend, an iron-fisted, no-nonsense tutor named Sue Lambiotte. She agreed to teach him—for free—while he was locked up and then, after he got out, six hours a day, five days a week. If he did not pass certain tests, Allen would not be allowed to graduate high school. And if he did not finish high school, he could not go to college to play ball.

So, for six months, Allen went to Lambiotte's home. He studied all the subjects he had ignored in school. He came for the last time on September 2, 1994, when he passed his final test. Lambiotte had a graduation ceremony that day, just she and Allen. He was the star student. He was going to college.

Allen's mom chose the school. While Allen was still in prison, Anne Iverson called up Georgetown University Coach John Thompson. He was one of the top coaches in the country. And he was known for being a no-nonsense leader who demanded the most from his players.

"I need my boy to have a strong coach who can guide him in the right direction," Anne Iverson said. "You're the only man who can do that. Will you please take my son?"

Thompson had seen Iverson play in high school and knew he could be a star. Plus, he was impressed with Anne Iverson's plea. He agreed to take on Allen, as long as Allen promised to follow the same rules and accomplish the same things in the classroom as everyone else. All coaches say that; John Thompson usually got it done.

Allen Iverson's mother, Anne, believed that Georgetown Head Coach John Thompson (above) was just the kind of coach and teacher that her son needed when he was considering which college to attend.

That fall, Allen Iverson left Virginia for Georgetown, which is in Washington, D.C. He rode away in the car and waved to his mother and sisters as they got smaller in the rear window. When the car turned the corner, he wept.

Leaving home was tough. But it was the start of a new, brighter chapter in his life.

Chapter 3

From Georgetown to the Pros

College was a whole new game for Allen Iverson. First, he was rusty from not having played organized ball in eighteen months. Second, the players he faced were far better than any he had seen in high school. He could no longer expect to beat five guys just by himself. His coach, John Thompson, would not even let him try.

His first game was against the defending national champion Arkansas Razorbacks in December 1994. The rust really showed. He committed two fouls and two turnovers in the first three minutes. He shot just 27 percent. Georgetown lost big.

But his talent still showed, even through the mistakes. His ball-handling was slick and his speed was dazzling. Most impressive was his nerve. Usually a freshman guard advances up court in a cautious hurry, shielding his dribble against anyone within ten feet of him. Iverson strutted straight at the national champs, bouncing the ball around his ears, daring anyone to try to steal it. Or he crossed half-court in a blink and hit the Arkansas zone like a marble rolling downhill. He was not scared by the top-ranked team in the country.

Arkansas coach Nolan Richardson was breathless. "I've seen three calf shows and nine horse ropings," Richardson said. "I even saw Elvis Presley once. But I've never seen a guard do what he can do with the basketball. I saw him go through traps of ours nobody's ever gone through. He's awesome. Wait until he starts playing."

Clearly, Iverson was a project that Coach Thompson had to mold. He had a habit of outrunning his teammates, which left him playing a lot of one-on-five. The coach, to break the habit, stopped practice one day and made his point by formally introducing Iverson to center Othella Harrington, forward Jahidi White, and his other teammates on the court. Thompson also forced Iverson to play defense, something he had ignored back in high school. Quickly enough, Iverson's defense improved to where it sometimes outshined his offense. He finished fourth in the nation in steals as a freshman.

Thompson realized he had a special talent in Iverson. The youngster combined the quickness of Kenny Anderson, the shiftiness of Isaiah Thomas, and the shooting range of Mark Price. Some said he was the most exciting player college basketball had seen since Pistol Pete Maravich played at Louisiana State University in the 1960s. So, often enough, Thompson just gave Iverson the ball and basically said, "Do with it what you may." And Iverson did.

"I want the ball at game's end," said Iverson. "My coach hollers at me when I don't have it."

Late in the season, the Georgetown Hoyas faced off against the St. John's University Red Storm, who were led by another spectacular freshman, Felipe Lopez. It was a nationally televised game, billed as a meeting between two future NBA superstars.

Iverson played the game on a sprained ankle. It did not really matter. While Lopez struggled against Georgetown's bump-and-thump defense, Iverson ignited the Hoyas' offense. At one point he faked a behind-the-back pass on a break and kept the ball himself for an easy two. Another time he juked going around befuddled St. John's defender Mo Brown and pulled up for a liquid-smooth jumper. Georgetown won the game; Iverson easily won the showdown with Lopez.

Iverson finished the season averaging a team-leading 20.4 points per game. He was also named the top defensive player in the Big East Conference, which was made up of ten of the nation's best basketball programs. Georgetown won twenty-one games, lost just ten, and finished in the final sixteen in the NCAA championships.

The next season was even better. Iverson averaged 25.6 points per game. He was named the Most Valuable Player in the Big East, which he led in points and steals. The Hoyas went 29–8, advancing to the NCAA's Elite Eight.

Around the country, college basketball fans would throw up their hands in amazement at his latest moves. They would ask each other: Did you see him pour in 40 against Seton Hall? Can you believe how he picked Miami's pocket for 10 steals in a single game?

Iverson had one of his best nights against a tough Villanova University squad. Nova guard Kerry Kittles—himself an All-American—tried to guard Iverson. No chance. Iverson blew past Kittles repeatedly, or played Kittles like a yo-yo, getting him to dive for the ball before pulling it back for a nothing-but-net jumper. Once, Iverson drove through the middle, only to be clubbed on the head by Villanova center Jason Lawson. As he tumbled to the floor, Iverson pushed up a prayer of a shot that gently swished through the twine. He finished the play by sinking the foul shot. Iverson ended the game with 37 points, as the Hoyas topped the Nova Wildcats.

After the season, Iverson had a tough decision to make.

Should he stay in college or go pro? Few of John Thompson's players ever left before four full years on campus. But Iverson was already considered by many to be the nation's top college player. If he went to the NBA, he would likely be the first player selected in the annual draft of college players. He would make millions of dollars. What should he do?

The decision came down to one issue: his family. Iverson's mother and sisters had lived in poverty for years. So it really was an easy decision. By going pro, Iverson could make sure his family lived in a nice home and had enough food on the table. He told Coach Thompson of his decision. The coach agreed that Iverson was making the right choice.

In May 1996, the NBA held its annual draft lottery. Ping-Pong balls carrying the logos of the league's thirteen worst teams were put into a hopper. One would be pulled out. The team whose logo was on that ball would get the first choice of all players coming out of college that spring.

The question was: who would get the top pick? There was little doubt, however, as to who the first pick would be.

NBA Commissioner David Stern announced the results on national television. When the lucky Ping-Pong ball went to the Philadelphia 76ers, team President Pat Croce leaped from his chair. He began high-fiving stunned officials from other teams. Croce made no attempt to hide who he would take in the draft. "Allen is unbelievable," he said. "This is what it's all about. Being excited about something you believe in." He compared Iverson to another rookie who had taken the NBA by storm back in 1984, one Michael Jordan. "Allen," said Croce, "is the answer."

The answer, or "The Answer"? It is not clear which Croce meant. You see, Iverson picked up the nickname The Answer back in his youth. The story goes that when a key basket was needed, or a crucial touchdown in football, Iverson was the answer. "It's just something guys around the neighborhood started calling me and it stuck," Iverson

Allen Iverson poses with a Philadelphia 76ers jersey shortly after the team selected him as the first overall pick in the 1996 NBA Draft.

said. Today, he sports a tattoo of a bulldog with the words "The Answer" on his left bicep.

But was he The Answer in the NBA? Lots of hot-shot players come out of college and fail in the pros. The game is faster, the players bigger and tougher, the life more demanding. As good as he was at Georgetown, Iverson was no sure bet in Philadelphia.

The rookie served notice quickly. In a November game against the New York Knicks, Iverson was covered by Knicks guard Charlie Ward. He started rocking and rolling. The Knicks' scouting report told Ward that Iverson liked to go right. When he faked left, Ward still bit, and Iverson went past him to the right as if Ward were a stone statue. The sellout crowd in Philadelphia's Core States Arena went "Ooooooh." Iverson did not even make the layup because he ran into Patrick Ewing in front of the basket. But the move was so good they showed it on the replay board. A replay of a miss.

Pictured at left is a photo of Iverson's left arm with its many tattoos.

Iverson pulls up for a jump shot against the Cleveland Cavaliers.

He fouled out both Ward and Knicks guard Scott Brooks in that game, scoring 35 points.

The NBA had a new star attraction.

As the season went on, he only got better. In April, he scored 40 or more points in five straight games. No rookie in league history had ever done that. Against the Cleveland Cavaliers, he scored 50 points, becoming—at twenty-one years and 310 days—the second youngest player ever to hit that mark.

At season's end, Iverson averaged 23.5 points per game, along with 7.5 rebounds. Those stats were better than the rookie seasons of some of the best point guards ever, including Isaiah Thomas, Magic Johnson, and Bob Cousy. They were enough to earn him the award of NBA Rookie of the Year.

But they were not enough to make the 76ers a good team. Philadelphia finished with a record of 22 wins and 60 losses. At season's end, the team traded six players—half of their roster. Coach Johnny Davis was fired.

In Davis's place, the Sixers hired Larry Brown, a veteran who had coached five other NBA teams. Brown was a winner—he had had 23 winning seasons in 25 years of coaching college and pros. But, perhaps more importantly, he had once been an undersized and scrappy point guard. If anyone could teach Iverson how to win, it was Brown.

The first thing Coach Brown asked Iverson was what he wanted from his coach. "Allen said all he wanted was one person who believed in him," Brown said. "I'm that person."

Perhaps. But it would not always be that easy.

Chapter 4

Coach Brown

In some ways, Allen Iverson and Larry Brown are quite different. Brown is an old-school coach. His players are expected to hustle on defense and play a controlled game on offense. Iverson is a new-style player. His style was always shoot, shoot again and—if you miss—keep shooting until it goes in. Defense? That was supposed to be some-body else's job.

Brown is a conservative man. He dresses neatly in suits and ties. He speaks softly—but powerfully. When he calls a practice for 2:00 P.M., he expects his players to be there no later than 1:30 P.M. Iverson is of the hip-hop generation. He dresses in loud clothes, fancy jewelry, and doo-rags. He speaks softly, but his rap is loud. An afternoon practice? Not if it can be avoided. Iverson prefers to save his energy for the real games.

In other ways, Allen Iverson and Larry Brown are quite the same.

Both were raised by single mothers. Both were the smallest guys every time they ran onto the basketball court. Back in his days as a point guard in the old American Basketball Association (ABA), Brown became famous for hurling his 165-pound body into the mass of giants. That is exactly the style that Iverson plays today.

Both Brown and Iverson are easily insulted. Both often feel misunderstood. And both knew that for the

Philadelphia 76ers to succeed, they would have to learn to appreciate their similarities and work out their differences. Each needed the other, or they had no chance of doing what they both wanted to do: win. Winning is everything.

From their very first practices together in 1997, it became clear that the coach saw Iverson as his special project. The Sixers were streaking up and down the court in three-on-three drills. Brown only had eyes—and instructions—for one man.

"Allen, go down the lane sooner," Brown urged. "Allen, get to your position sooner. Space out. Don't get caught out of position."

Iverson nodded toward the coach and hustled down the floor. Only when Brown finished with the lesson did Iverson relax with a few hip-hop dance steps and friendly high-fives.

Would the tough lessons work? In some ways, yes. The Sixers were an improved team in 1997–98. Brown's "defense-first" approach brought them nine more wins than they had the season before. And there was a sense that the team was finally moving in the right direction. Brown and Sixers general manager Billy King made trade after trade to improve the talent around Iverson. In came veteran defender George Lynch and talented swingman Aaron McKie. Out went players who did not show hustle every time they entered the game.

But in other ways Brown and Iverson quickly rubbed each other's nerves raw. The coach was looking for a controlled style of play. That meant lots of passes before taking a shot. It meant slowing down the game to wait for teammates.

"Sometimes you run down and jack up a bad shot and nobody else touches the ball," Brown told Iverson one day. "What good have you done? Your teammates get tired of covering for you on defense. They don't want to set a good

Allen Iverson receives instructions from Sixers Head Coach Larry Brown during a timeout.

screen for you. If you don't get them involved, it gets old for them real fast."

Iverson had been allowed total freedom under Coach Thompson and Coach Davis. He wanted to use his speed and his moves. He did not like waiting for anyone—even teammates. Sometimes, he even liked hot-dogging a little bit when the cameras were on him.

There was the game against the Orlando Magic when the Sixers were about to bust the game open. They had a three-on-one break. Iverson had the ball. He brought it behind his back, then tried to flip it to the wing. Instead, he lost the ball to the lone Magic defender, Bo Outlaw. That created a four-on-two at the other end and a four-point screw-up. The Sixers lost by seven.

"He tried something for the television highlights instead of just making the bucket," groaned Coach Brown. "All of a sudden it's degree-of-difficulty time."

For his part, Iverson felt stung every time Brown criticized him publicly. Allen Iverson is a sensitive young man. He did not mind taking advice from his coach. But he wondered why the coach went to reporters rather than talking straight to him. When he felt insulted, he sulked. When he sulked, his play would suffer. In a game after an argument between the two men, Iverson shot 2-for-17 in a loss to the Denver Nuggets.

Other nights, it would all come together. In a game against the Houston Rockets during his second season, Iverson was nearly perfect. He scored 26 points in a combination of swooping dunks, courageous drives to the hoop, and fade-away jumpers. He involved his teammates, getting 15 assists. On one play, Iverson cut through the lane and suddenly stopped, causing Rockets guard Clyde Drexler to trip over his own feet. While other defenders scrambled to defend Iverson, he slipped a nifty touch pass

Iverson dunks the ball during a game against the Los Angeles Clippers on February 25, 1997.

to teammate Tim Thomas, who tipped it in for an easy two points.

At season's end, Iverson averaged 22 points per game, down slightly from his rookie season. But he made 46 percent of his shots, up from 41 percent the year before. The 76ers were building around Iverson, and slowly becoming a better team. Clearly, he was one of the National Basketball Association's rising stars.

He was also one of its more controversial players. A lot of that controversy centered on his looks.

The first thing you notice on Allen Iverson is his tattoos. From his neck to his ankles, much of his 165-pound body is covered with artwork and words. On his arms are tributes to family and friends. In addition to the tattoo on his bicep, he also has "The Answer" tattooed on his chest. On his neck are Chinese letters spelling out the word "loyalty."

Keep looking. You will see Iverson's hair—that is, if he is not wearing a do-rag. Iverson sports the fanciest corn-rows ever seen. A hairdresser comes to his house twice a week. She spends more than an hour putting his braids into waves, squares, zig-zags, or whatever pattern fits his mood. Iverson usually refuses to be seen or to be interviewed on camera if his cornrows are not exactly as he likes them. Then look at his clothes: Baggy jeans, a long T-shirt, and a double-oversized leather jacket. If you were to walk a mile in Iverson's shoes, you might trip, because he rarely ties his laces.

Even on the court, Iverson dresses differently. The league has warned him about having his uniform shorts too long and complained that his ankle braces cover up his white socks. NBA Commissioner David Stern was upset when Iverson showed up in a white skullcap to get his 1996–97 Rookie of the Year trophy. "Some people want me to wear Italian suits all the time like Michael Jordan,"

Iverson dribbles around a defender in a game against the Dallas Mavericks on November 13, 1997.

Iverson said. "But I'm not Michael Jordan. I'm a younger guy. I'm a different generation. Don't rush me."

The arguments about Iverson's looks have often been along age lines. Many adults look at his style and his swagger and think he must be a troublemaker. He hears their anger in the NBA arenas. In Orlando one night, a man in the fourth row hollered, "Hey, crack boy! Go back to jail!" In New York, an older fan yelled, "I can't believe they let you play in this league." Even in Philadelphia he hears shouts of, "Get a haircut!"

But those shouts almost never come from younger people. To many of them, Iverson represents the future of style. If their parents do not always understand, well, that is okay.

"You know, I see Allen in his huge baggy pants and the untied boots, everything untucked," said Sixers announcer Steve Mix, a fine player himself some thirty years ago. "I think, oh man, look at this guy. Then I go home and see my eleven-year-old wearing the exact same stuff. I mean, people see Allen and are scared of him, but is he any different from other kids of his generation?"

He is different in one way—he is a millionaire. That has allowed Iverson to add layer upon layer of gold and diamonds to his look. His jewelry costs more than most people's houses. If that bothers people, he does not care. He says the desire to own such fancy things came from a childhood spent in poverty. Back when the power was shut off to his boyhood home, he and his mom sat in the dark and dreamed of the fancy jewelry they might own one day. Now that he has arrived, he is not about to forget the dream.

Iverson loves the fans who attend his games. Still, he feels closer to the people who cannot afford to spend $40 to see the NBA. Many of the people who regard him as a hero are not in the seats. They're home watching on television or shivering outside the arena, waiting to catch a glimpse of

Iverson in his car as he drives away after the game. It is the poor people to whom Iverson feels the closest.

"I'm proud to represent them," he says. "They're with me because I come from where they come from. They can understand why I dress the way I dress, why I wear my hair the way I wear my hair. So they respect me and love me. They know the odds against someone like me making it."

There is no doubt that Iverson had made it by the age of twenty-three. The next question is whether he could help a team make it. To be considered a true superstar, he would have to turn the Sixers into a winner. That would start in 1999.

Chapter 5

The Answer

The city of Philadelphia has one of America's best basketball traditions. Wilt Chamberlain grew up there and later played pro ball for two Philadelphia teams, the Warriors and the 76ers. Chamberlain led the Sixers to an NBA title. Until Michael Jordan came along, the seven-foot Wilt was regarded as the best player in history.

After Wilt Chamberlain came Julius Erving—the flying "Doctor J"—who led the Sixers to an NBA championship. And after Erving came Charles Barkley, who led the team in scoring, rebounds, and outrageous remarks during his eight years in the City of Brotherly Love.

But when Barkley was traded away in 1992, Philadelphia turned into the City of Losing Basketball. The Sixers missed the playoffs for seven straight years. The fans knew what was needed: someone who could carry the team as Wilt, Doc, and Charles had done before.

In 1998–99, Allen Iverson became that man.

Several things led to the growth. First, Larry Brown switched Iverson's position. The coach moved Iverson from point guard to shooting guard. That meant he no longer had to dribble the ball up the court. It freed him up to look for better scoring chances.

Second, the Sixers continued to add good players. Eric Snow came from the Seattle Supersonics to play point guard. Theo Ratliff arrived from the Detroit Pistons to bring defense and rebounding.

Third, Iverson continued to mature.

"I came into this league knowing I had a lot to learn," Iverson said. "I just wanted to learn it all right away. I found out that you can't rush things. You just have to keep working. Now I'm realizing what it takes, as a player and as a man."

Iverson averaged 26.8 points per game in 1998–99 —tops in the league. Standing less than six feet tall, he was the shortest player in NBA history to accomplish that feat. That year, he finished fourth in voting for Most Valuable Player.

More importantly, the 76ers finally made the playoffs.

It is the fourth game of the 1999 opening round playoff game between the 76ers and Orlando Magic. Iverson is looking toward the upper reaches of the First Union Center in Philadelphia. He has his right hand cupped to his ear. It is a signal to get louder, and more than 19,000 fans oblige. There is now a love between Allen Iverson and Philadelphia's fans.

The Sixers, up two games to one in the series, shoot off to an early lead. Iverson is on fire. In the first five minutes, he buries a fifteen-footer, sinks two free throws, tosses in a running twelve-footer, and sinks another free throw. This creates wild joy in the stands, on his bench, and on the floor.

Iverson feeds off a crowd as much as any athlete who has ever played. The noise acts as a pick-me-up for him. When he waves his arms or cups his ear (pretending not to hear), the fans respond. As they go wild, he plays that much better.

Orlando's Anfernee Hardaway is trying to guard Iverson. Although he is seven inches taller, Hardaway has no chance. Iverson gets him one-on-one. He dips, gives a

Allen Iverson signals for the home crowd to make some noise during a playoff game against the Orlando Magic in Philadelphia on May 15, 1999.

head fake to the left, and speeds past Hardaway on the right side. Hardaway stands flat footed. Iverson then jumps—it is almost like he is floating—reaching his long arms over Magic forward Nick Anderson. The ball rolls off Iverson's fingertips, wafts past Armstrong's outstretched arm, and gently lands in the basket for another two.

The fans go nuts. Keith Ennis, a thirty-year-old wearing a No. 3 Iverson jersey, jumps up in the stands. "He plays so big, but he comes in such a little package," Ennis says. "The high school kids look at him and say, 'Hey, I'm bigger than that.' That's why they relate to him so well. Allen transcends any race, creed, or color."

The Sixers won the game, 101–91. They also won the series, three games to one.

They made a valiant run into the second round of the playoffs. Then the veteran Indiana Pacers knocked Iverson's body around and took the Sixers out in four games. Iverson never whined, never complained. He just kept getting back up every time he was slammed down by the bigger bodies.

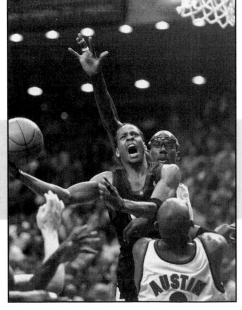

Iverson takes the ball to the hoop against Orlando Magic defender Isaac Austin in a playoff game on May 11, 1999.

Philadelphia's fans ate this up. Not the battering Iverson endured, but the effort he gave, the guts he showed.

You want to be a fan of Allen Iverson? That is something worth being. He puts on a show. He gives every last ounce of sweat. He is a soaring spirit—a gifted survivor. He feeds off all the support he can get.

He is also a human highlight film. No player in NBA history has ever been faster. Few have shown his talent with the ball. In 1998, the magazine *Sports Illustrated* asked players who they thought had the best ball-handling move in the league. Kobe Bryant of the Los Angeles Lakers got some votes. So did Damon Stoudamire of the Portland Trail Blazers and Rod Strickland of the Washington Wizards. But Allen Iverson's crossover dribble was easily voted the best move around.

The crossover is based on speed and surprise. Iverson walks toward his defender. He switches the dribble from his right hand to his left and back again, over and over. Finally the defender runs out of patience and lunges for the ball. In a flash, Iverson crosses it over to the other hand and he is gone. The move is so good that one time, Iverson brought the great Michael Jordan to his knees when Jordan tried to stop him.

"If it's about oohs and aahs, it's about Allen," said Sixers Assistant Coach Gar Heard. "It's like art."

There were many more oohs and aahs in the 1999–2000 season. The Sixers, after their success the year before, did not catch anyone by surprise this time. Iverson drew more double-teams from opponents, who vowed not to let the little man beat them. Still, he did beat them and the Sixers kept winning. Iverson upped his scoring average to 28.4 points per game, second in the NBA to Shaquille O'Neal. And the Sixers won 49 regular-season games, their highest total in ten years.

Iverson flashes his famous crossover-dribble move in a game against the Seattle Supersonics on January 21, 2002.

Coach Brown had added a few more pieces to the puzzle. Tyrone Hill, a lanky rebounder, came from the Milwaukee Bucks. And Toni Kukoc came from the Chicago Bulls. Kukoc was a good outside shooter whom the coach thought might force teams to stop double-teaming Iverson.

Double-team or triple-team him, Iverson just kept scoring. He also ranked third in the NBA in minutes played and third in steals. The league's fans voted him a starter in the NBA All-Star Game. He was the first 76er since Charles Barkley in 1992 to receive that honor. Iverson starred in the 2000 All-Star Game, leading all scorers with 26 points.

The team and its star were now getting respect and attention. Late in the season, national TV carried a game between the Sixers and the Toronto Raptors. Toronto had an exciting star player, Vince Carter, who rivaled Iverson as a highlight maker. The two young teams were tied near the top of the Eastern Conference standings.

Iverson considered Carter a bit of a rival among the NBA's young stars. He wanted to have a big game before a big television audience. He wanted to show that the man nicknamed The Answer was better than the man nick-named Air Canada.

His plan did not work in the first half. Iverson had just 13 points on 5-of-12 shooting. Then the third quarter arrived, and The Answer left the Raptors with nothing but questions on how to stop him. Doug Christie tried sticking to Iverson but could not defend his quickness. The five-foot-three Muggsy Bogues was next, but Iverson pulled up right in his face. Carter and Tracy McGrady tried, but Iverson either got fouled or flat-out drove past them.

He attacked the basket. Then he made the free throws. Then, after a hard foul from Charles Oakley sent him to the floor, Iverson got up and walked it off. A jumper fol-lowed seven seconds later. Then a three-point conversion.

Iverson goes in for a lay-up against the Toronto Raptors Vince Carter (15).

Then a driving layup and two more free throws. By the time the third quarter ended, Iverson had 28 points.

And he was not done. Iverson added 16 points in the fourth quarter, including a jumper that ignited a pivotal 7–0 run that put the Sixers up for good. After that, Vince Carter left the floor with his head bowed in defeat. Iverson's message was loud and clear: "This is my house."

"The basket was like an ocean tonight," Iverson said after his 44-point night. "I was just ready. When a quality player like Vince comes in, I want to help my team as much as he does. I felt he was coming into my house. I wanted to turn it up."

The Sixers turned it up right into the 2000 playoffs. They beat the Charlotte Hornets, three games to one, in the first round. Then they faced the Indiana Pacers for the second straight post-season. The year before, Indiana had sent the Sixers home in four straight games. This time, the Sixers won two games before bowing out to Reggie Miller and his Pacer teammates.

Iverson believed the team was improving. He was looking forward to the 2000–01 season. One more year together, he thought, and the 76ers could take a big step forward. Perhaps they could even get as far as the NBA Finals. That was his dream.

Then Iverson was rudely awakened from his dream. A few weeks after he went home to rest for the summer, he got a call from Pat Croce. The Sixers president told Iverson that the team was planning to trade him. They were discussing deals to send him to the Detroit Pistons or the Los Angeles Clippers.

Iverson was floored. "The Clippers?" he said. "Nobody wants to play for the Clippers."

At first, he was angry. Then he decided to look at it another way. If the Sixers wanted to trade him, he must have given them a reason. What had he done wrong?

Chapter 6

MVP!

After learning that he might be traded, Allen Iverson sat down with Sixers coach Larry Brown and team president Pat Croce. The three men cleared the air. Brown told Iverson he was tired of having his star player miss practices. Croce said he was disappointed that Iverson was always the last player to arrive for games and the first to leave after they ended. Brown added that Iverson's teammates often felt that he was selfish with the ball.

Iverson, too, had his complaints. He felt the coach often treated him like a child. Sometimes, Iverson said, Brown seemed to try to embarrass him in front of his teammates. He wanted to be treated with respect.

"To get respect," Brown said, "you must give respect."

Iverson heard the words. He did not want to leave Philadelphia. He liked the city and its fans. He enjoyed his teammates and believed the 76ers were on the verge of becoming a great team.

So he promised to change. If the Sixers did not trade him, he would come to practice each day and arrive early for games. He would set an example for his teammates. He would give respect and act professional.

The trade was called off. And Coach Brown, to show his good faith, named Iverson co-captain of the 2000–01 Sixers, along with point guard Eric Snow.

"Allen told me more that he wants to have a relationship like Magic Johnson had with Coach Pat Riley, like Michael Jordan had with Coach Phil Jackson," Brown said. "I still do not like Iverson's music or the way he dresses. But Iverson has a lot of good in him and I'm finding it out every single day. I'm watching him grow up as a person and feel good about himself."

The Sixers felt good about themselves as the new season started. Led by Iverson, they won their first ten games. It was the best start in the history of the franchise. Iverson's scoring was down a bit, but that was because he was sharing the ball more. One night, against the New York Knicks at Madison Square Garden, Iverson even jumped on forward Tyrone Hill for failing to run a play—for Hill, not himself.

Iverson kept working on his behavior and attitude. "I'm not perfect," he said. "But I am trying every day to concentrate on being a better basketball player and a better person."

Better player? Hard to imagine. Give him the ball, and he will create a way to score. He can hit the three, drain fifteen-foot jumpers, or stop defenders in their tracks with his lightning-quick crossover dribble. Despite his small frame, he has a forty-one-inch vertical leap and a seven-foot wingspan. He is so quick that he makes the best defenders look as if they were stuck in quicksand.

As the season progressed, he was late for only one practice—and he called ahead of time to let the team know. He was respectful of the coaches and their rules. His play and his behavior were so impressive that he was voted a starter in the 2001 All-Star Game. He scored 22 points and was voted the game's Most Valuable Player.

Ask Allen Iverson what he wants fans to see in his game and he answers in one word: Courage.

That is easy to see in any game. Iverson gets knocked

Iverson poses with his new teammate, Dikembe Mutombo (55), in 2001.

Actually, the first series was not that tough. The Indiana Pacers had sent the Sixers home from the playoffs the past two years. This time, the Sixers knocked off the Indiana Pacers three games to one. The Sixers lost the first game of the series. In Game Two, however, Iverson shot 15-for-27 and pumped in 45 points. After that performance, the Pacers never really challenged again.

Next up was the Toronto Raptors, led by Vince Carter. Once again, the Sixers lost the first game. Carter scored 35 to beat the Sixers in Philadelphia.

Iverson hated losing, especially before his home crowd. He came out ready for Game Two at Philadelphia's First Union Center. He scored 35 points in the first three quarters. Still, the 76ers led by just two with less than four minutes to play. Then Iverson really took over.

He gave the Sixers breathing room by hitting a short bank shot and then making two free throws for an 89–84 lead with 3:49 left. The sellout crowd of 20,870 chanted "MVP, MVP!"

A minute later, Iverson hit a running jumper, got fouled, and completed the three-point play. That gave the Sixers a six-point lead.

After Toronto's Charles Oakley nailed a three-pointer, Iverson drilled an eighteen-footer to make it 94–89. Following a miss by the Raptors, Iverson got fouled. He cupped his ear, signaling the crowd to make more noise. He screamed toward the sky. He made both free throws, clinching the game.

When they added up the numbers, Iverson had scored 54 points that night. It broke the team's playoff scoring record of 50, set by Hall of Famer Billy Cunningham.

"They've been pumping Allen up as the next superstar in the league," said Sixers teammate Aaron McKie. "They say he's the next guy to carry the torch. Well, he's getting it and running with it."

Allen Iverson blows by Shaquille O'Neal (34) of the Los Angeles Lakers.

Then he hit a jumper over Lakers defender Derek Fisher with 48 seconds to go to make it 103–99.

Then he swished two foul shots with 25 seconds to go to clinch the win, 107–101.

For one night, at least, the Sixers proved they could hang with—indeed, beat—the world's best basketball team. Ultimately, the Lakers won the series, four games to one. But Iverson and his teammates went home with their heads high. It had been an amazing year. The season started with Iverson nearly being traded away; it ended with him being voted the league's top player and leading his team to the championship round.

In a lot of ways, that sums up Allen Iverson's life. He has made mistakes and been in trouble. He is far from perfect. But he has worked hard, in basketball and in the real world, to improve himself. He keeps working, day after day, to be a better player and a better person.

"I've learned a lot in the last few years," he said recently. "I know I've got a long way to go. But I'm proud of how far I've come."

It is unclear whether he was talking about Allen Iverson as a basketball player or as a man. Most likely, he was talking about both.

Career Statistics

College

Season	Team	GP	FG%	REB	PTS	PPG
1994–1995	Georgetown	30	.390	99	134	20.4
1995–1996	Georgetown	37	.480	141	173	25.0
Totals		67	.440	240	307	23.0

NBA

Season	Team	GP	FG%	REB	AST	STL	BLK	PTS	PPG
1996–1997	Philadelphia	76	.416	312	567	157	24	1,787	23.5
1997–1998	Philadelphia	80	.461	296	494	176	25	1,758	22.0
1998–1999	Philadelphia	48	.412	236	223	110	7	1,284	26.8
1999–2000	Philadelphia	70	.421	267	328	144	5	1,989	28.4
2000–2001	Philadelphia	71	.420	273	325	178	20	2,207	31.1
2001–2002	Philadelphia	60	.398	269	331	168	13	1,883	31.4
Totals		405	.421	1,653	2,268	933	94	10,908	26.9

GP=Games Played   AST=Assists   PTS=Points scored
FG%=Field Goal Percentage   STL=Steals   PPG=Points per game
REB=Rebounds   BLK=Blocks

Where to Write
Allen Iverson:

Mr. Allen Iverson
c/o The Philadelphia 76ers
First Union Center Complex
3601 S. Broad Street
Philadelphia, PA 19148

On the Internet at:

http://www.nba.com/playerfile/allen_iverson/index.
html?nav=page

http://www.nba.com/sixers

Index